Dirty Jokes
Over 100 Sex Jokes

R. J. Clarke

Dirty Jokes

What should you do if your girlfriend starts smoking during sex?
Slow down and use some lubricant

What do you call a man who cries when he masturbates?
A tearjerker

What happens when you get naked in the bathroom?
The shower gets turned on

How do you make herb bread
With a dill dough

What do you call two men fighting over a slut?
Tug of whore

Why was the snowman happy?
Because he heard that the snowblower was coming

What do you call a chameleon that can't have sex?
A reptile dysfunction

Why is a woman's mind cleaner than a man's?
Because they change it more often

What is Impotence?
Nature's way of saying no hard feelings

Why shouldn't you blame a nudist for being the way they are?
Because they were born that way

What is the most common sleeping position of a slut?
Around

Why did the semen cross the road?
Because I put on the wrong socks today

Who is the most popular guy in a nudist colony?
The guy who can hold a cup of coffee in each hand and a dozen donuts

How can you tell if a girl is ticklish?
Give her a test-tickle

Why did the man cancel his appointment at the sperm clinic?
Because he couldn't cum

What did the guy with no dick give to his wife?
A good bollocking

How do you know if you're in a same sex relationship?
The sex is always the same

Why is a woman like a casino?
Liquor in the front and poker in the back

What's worse than waking up and finding a penis drawn on your face?
Finding out it was traced

Have you ever had sex while camping?
It's fucking intense

What do you get if you cross a penis with a potato?
A dick-tater

Do you know what a 6.9 is?
A good thing that's ruined by a period

Why is sex like playing a game of Bridge
Because if you don't have a good partner, you'd better have a good hand

What do you call someone with a one inch dick?
Justin

Why do they call it the Wonder Bra?
Because when you take the bra off, you wonder where the boobs went

What do you call a cheap circumcision?
A rip off

What compliment did the midget say that caused great offense?
Your hair smells nice

Have you heard about the person who is gay and dyslexic?
He's still in Daniel

Why do nurses give old men Viagra at night?
Because it stops them from rolling out of bed

What did the bra say to the hat?
You go on a head and I'll give these two a lift

What do you get if you cross a flea with a chicken?
An itchy cock

What's long, hard and has cum in it?
Cucumber

Why was the man so terrible at foreplay
Because he was a bit out of touch

What do you call the space between Pamela Anderson's breasts?
Silicon Valley

What did the mother say when her daughter asked her how to spell penis?
You should have asked me last night, it was at the tip of my tongue

What type of bees produce milk?
Boobies

What do you call a nurse with dirty knees?
The head nurse

Why is sex like math?
Because you add a bed, subtract the clothes, divide the legs and then multiply

Why do the ladies love Jesus?
Because he's hung like this… (spread arms out)

What brand label is on a prostitute's knickers
NEXT

What's long, hard and full of seamen?
A submarine

How can you tell if a man is dead?
Because he's stiff for longer than 2 minutes

What do you call a midget orgy?
A little get together

What's the difference between a hooker and a drug dealer?
A hooker can wash her crack and sell it again

What's the difference between a genealogist and a gynecologist?
A genealogist checks the family tree whilst a gynecologist checks the family bush

What's 6 inches long and drives women wild?
A $100 bill

What did the man say when a woman asked, "What's up?"
If I tell you, will you sit on it

Why do men have a hole at the end of their penis?
Because it enables them to be open minded

What is a transvestite?
A guy who likes to eat, drink and be Mary

What do you call a herd of masturbating cows?
Beef strokin' off

What happened when two gay guys had an argument?
They exchanged blows

Can you get AIDS from a toilet seat?
You can if you sit down before the last guy gets up

What happens if a Viagra tablet gets stuck in your throat?
You get a stiff neck

How do you find a blind man on a nudist beach?
It's not hard

Arnold Schwarzenegger has a big one, Madonna doesn't have one and the Pope has one but doesn't use it. What is it?
A last name – what were you thinking of?

What do you call a police officer who shaved her pubes yesterday?
Cunt stubble

What did Cinderella do when she got to the ball?
She gagged

What do you call a marathon with just transvestites?
A drag race

How can four gay men sit on one stool?
Turn it upside down

Why did the accountant get a tattoo of money on his penis?
Because he likes to see his money grow

Why do women prefer old gynecologists?
Because they have shaky hands

What do you call an artist with a brown finger?
Picassole

How did the easily frightened man get an erection?
He was scared stiff

What did the Egyptian guy name his vehicle recovery business?
Camel Tow

What did the psychologist say to the man who was having marital problems?
I would recommend doing something sexy to a tractor

Why don't professional wrestlers have sex before a fight?
Probably because the wrestlers aren't attracted to each other

What happened to the prostitute who was working in a brothel?
She got laid off

What happened when the guy fell asleep in a bath tub?
He had a wet dream

Why are men like spiders?
Because when they are on the web, they get sticky hands

What happened after a blind man was doing a circumcision on a baby?
He got the sack

What did the sign say outside a brothel?
Beat it – we're closed

Can you rearrange these letters – PNEIS to spell an important body part when erect?
If you said spine then you are probably in the minority that have a clean mind

How do trees get pregnant?
By a woodpecker

What is the lightest thing in the world?
A penis because just a thought can raise it

What starts with the letter F and ends with uck?
Firetruck, what were you thinking of?

What is the cheapest meat?
Deer balls because they're under a buck

Why was the blonde's bellybutton bruised?
Because her boyfriend was blond

What is the difference between a blonde and a rooster?
In the morning, a rooster says, "Cock-a-doodle-doo" whilst a blonde says, "Any-cock'll-do"

What did the receptionist at a sperm clinic say to the man?
Thanks for coming

How do you know if your wife is a sex object?
If you ask her for sex, she objects

What do you call lesbian twins?
Lick-a-likes

Why do men get their best ideas when they are having sex?
Because they're plugged into a genius

What do you call a mailman after a sex change?
A post man

What did the blind man say when he walked past a fish market?
Good morning ladies

What do you call a nun after a sex change?
A transistor

Why did the woman masturbate with a mountaineer's ice pick?
Because she wanted to climb-axe

Have you heard about the guy who found out he was a test tube baby?

Now he knows for sure that his dad is a wanker

An elderly couple wanted to have children and decided it was best to see a doctor to see if it was possible. The doctor gave the man a jar and told him to come back tomorrow with a semen sample. The next day, the couple came to see the doctor and handed him an empty jar. The man explained, "I tried with my right hand, I then tried with my left hand and then my wife used both of her hands… but we still couldn't open the jar"

A man decided to go to a restaurant but it only served cheeseburgers for $2 and hand jobs for $10. The man asked the attractive lady behind the desk, "Are you the one that gives the hand jobs?" She replied proudly, "Yes, I am". The man then said, "In that case, can you wash your hands and make me a cheeseburger?"

I went to see my nurse for a check-up appointment and she told me that I must stop wanking. So I said, "Why is that, is it coz I'm going blind?" She replied, "No, it's because I'm trying to examine you"

Women who only like men with big dicks are shallow. In hindsight, that might not have been the best word to use

Three cash-strapped men went on a skiing vacation and to save some money they decided to sleep in the same bed. In the morning, the guy that was on the left side of the bed said, "I had a dream that I was getting a handjob". The guy that was on the right side of the bed said, "That's weird, I had the same dream". Then, the guy that slept in the middle said, "I had a dream that I was skiing"

Four nuns were standing in line at the pearly gates to heaven. St Peter asked the first nun if she had sinned. She said that she had looked at a penis so St Peter asked her to wash her eyes with holy water before entering heaven. The second nun said that she had held a penis so St Peter asked her to wash her hands in holy water before entering heaven. Then the fourth nun pushed in front of the third nun. St Peter asked, "Why did you do that?" She replied, "I want to gargle before she sits in it"

There was a sign in a window that read, "We are looking for a person to work with the chickens on our farm. Experience handling small cocks is required"

A woman comes home to find her husband in the bedroom. She says, "I want you to take off my boots". He slowly slips them off and his wife then asks, "Now I want you to take off my stockings". He gently slides them down and his wife then asks, "I want you to take off my bra". She then continues, "Now, if I catch you wearing my clothes again, I want a divorce"

A little girl had hurt her finger so she ran to her teacher and asked, "Can I have some cider for it?" The teacher replied, "Why do you need cider?" The girl replied, "I overheard my older sister say that when she has a prick in her hand, she puts it in cider"

An old woman said to her hard of hearing husband, "Would you like super sex tonight?" The man replied, "I'll have soup please"

An overweight guy was lazily watching TV until his interest perked when a commercial came on that guaranteed weight loss or your money back. The overweight guy decided to go with the $100 plan. The next day, a beautiful woman turned up at his door and said, "If you can catch me, you can have your way with me". After a week of running after her, the guy lost the guaranteed 10 pounds. He still wasn't happy with his body though so he decided to take the $200 plan, which guaranteed he'd lose a further 20 pounds. The next day, an even more beautiful woman turned up at his door. The man still wasn't happy with his body though so the next week he decided to go for the $1000 ultimate deluxe package which guaranteed extreme weight loss. When the box arrived at his door, a man popped out and said, "If I can catch you, I'll have my way with you"

My brother was so mean that he used to glue the pages of his porn magazines together so that I couldn't look at them

A mother told her daughter that if a boy touched her boobs, then she should say, "Don't". Her mother also told her that if a boy touched her pussy, then she should say, "Stop". Unfortunately, she met a boy who touched both, so she said, "Don't stop"

I went in to have a colonoscopy and was told to lie on my side and to pull my trousers down. The male nurse said, "Just to let you know, it's normal that during this type of procedure to get an erection". I replied, "I don't have an erection". The male nurse replied, "But I do"

A manager of a struggling business was unsure of who to sack but he knew it would have to be either Jack or Jill. So he waited to see who would come into work late the next day but they came in earlier than he did. He then waited to see who took an early lunchbreak but they both didn't take one, preferring to eat at their desk whilst they worked. At the end of the day, the manager approached Jill and said, "I have a problem, I am not sure whether to lay you or Jack off". Jill replied, "You had better jack off because I don't want to be late for my bus"

A woman had not long been playing golf when suddenly she got stung by a wasp. She ran into the clubhouse and asked for help. A gentleman asked, "Where did you get stung?" She replied, "Between the first and second hole". He said, "Your stance must be too wide"

A lonely man bought an inflatable sex doll for $10 from an adult store. When he started to use it, the doll began deflating so he decided to take it back to the shop to get a refund. He told the shopkeeper, "As soon as this sex doll was inflated, it started to go down on me". The shopkeeper replied, "Wow, I should be charging more for these"

Try saying the following sentence out loud five times: I won a math debate

A British man walks into a shop and asks, "Do you sell KY Jelly?". The shop assistant replied, "Sorry we don't have any of that here. Have you tried Boots?" The man angrily replied, "I'm trying to slide it in, not walk it in"

Peter's best friend at school asked him where he got his new Rolex watch from. Peter told him that his father gave it to him when he accidentally walked in on his parents having sex. Late at night, his best friend heard some noises in his parent's bedroom so he decided to walk in. His father shouted, "What do you want now?" The boy replied, "I wanna watch"

A man woke up in hospital and a nurse asked him what had happened. The man explained, "All I remember was that I was in an elevator with a very busty woman. I couldn't help but look at her tits and then she asked me to press one"

A young girl asked her grandad the question that every adult dreads, "What is sex?" The grandad decided to explain it as best as he could. After a while, he then asked, "What has caused this curiosity in this particular topic?" The young girl replied, "I didn't know what it meant when Grandma said that dinner will be ready in a few secs"

Tom and Lucy were visiting a zoo but they accidentally got locked inside a cage for the whole night. On the bright side, it was the first time they had mated successfully in captivity

If sex is a pain in the ass, you're doing it wrong

An old lady went to the dentist. When she sat down on the chair, she pulled her skirt down. The dentist said, "I'm not a gynecologist". She replied, "I know, I just want you to take my husband's teeth out"

Two nuns were waiting at the pearly gates. Saint Peter said that they must answer a question correctly in order to get into heaven. The first question he said was, "What were the names of the two people that lived in the Garden of Eden?" The first nun said, "Adam and Eve" and she was allowed into heaven. The second question was, "What was the first thing that Eve said when she saw Adam?" The second nun paused for thought and then said, "Boy, that's a hard one" and she was allowed into heaven

A teacher walked into her classroom and saw the word penis written on her blackboard. She didn't think much of it and rubbed it off. The next day, she saw the word penis in larger letters on the blackboard. She looked at her pupils, hoping to spot the guilty culprit and then she rubbed it off. The next day, she saw that the word penis was so large it took up the whole blackboard. She said, "Alright, who did it?" Nobody owned up. She then said, "I'm going to close my eyes for 10 seconds and I want the culprit to rub it off". A boy crept to the blackboard, rubbed it off and then wrote, "The more you rub it, the bigger it gets"

An Englishman, a Scotsman and a bear walk into a bar. The Englishman says, "I prefer English women". The Scotsman says, "I prefer Scottish women". Then the bear says, "I prefer bear women"

A scruffy looking man asked a taxi driver if he could drive him home. The taxi driver asked, "Do you have any money?" He replied, "Not on me but I can pay you when I get home". The taxi driver said, "Forget it" and drove off, leaving the man to walk home. The next day, the man decided to get some revenge. He saw a line of taxi drivers and asked them all, "Can you take me home and give me a blowjob for $20". One by one they all refused him. Then when he approached the taxi driver from yesterday, the man showed his $20 bill and said, "Can you drive me home?" The taxi driver let him in and then the man looked out of the window with a grin and put his two thumbs up as he passed the other taxi drivers

A man and women were having sex in the back seat of a car. The man then looked in the mirror and saw a cop walking towards him so he leapt into the driver's seat and drove off at full speed. This caused their clothes to fly out of the windows. Then as he approached a bend in the road, he noticed that his erect penis was jammed in the steering wheel. Unfortunately, he crashed and he was still stuck inside the car. He told the woman, "Go get some help". She said, "But I'm completely naked". The man found one of his shoes and told her to use it cover her vagina. She kept running until she found a doctor. She said, "You've got to help me, my boyfriend's trapped". He looked at the shoe and said, "I'm afraid that there's not much I can do, he's simply too far in"

A man was setting up an email account and decided to use 'mypenis' as a password. However, an error message popped up and said, "Not long enough"

A man returned home from the army and told his wife that he has trained his penis. She was curious and asked him to show her. He took his clothes off and shouted, "Attention" and his penis instantly stood erect. He then shouted, "At ease" and his penis instantly flopped down. His wife asked, "Can you do it again?" So the man shouted, "Attention" but his penis didn't go erect this time. He then started to masturbate and his wife said, "You don't have to do that". The man said, "I do because my penis disobeyed a direct order so I'm going to have to give it a dishonorable discharge"

A walrus takes his car to a garage to get it fixed. The mechanic says, "I think you blew a seal". The walrus replies, "I'd rather you didn't talk about my sex life, now what's wrong with my car?"

An American man walked into a hospital donation center and sat down on a chair next to a woman. He asked her, "What are you donating?" She replied, "I'm here to donate some blood because they give me $25". The man said, "I come here every week to donate sperm because they pay me $50". They both get called in and they see each other again the next week. The man said, "Are you here to donate some more blood again?" The woman shook her head because her mouth was full

A chicken and an egg were lying in bed. The chicken was smoking a cigarette with a huge grin on his face whilst the egg had a frown as she said, "Well that answers that question"

A vicar was staying the night in a hotel and asked the receptionist, "I hope the pornography channel is disabled". The receptionist gave a funny look and replied, "No, it's just normal porn you sick bastard"

An old woman goes into an adult store and sees a line of dildos of various shapes and sizes on a shelf. She then asks, "Can I have that big red one?" The man replied, "No, that's a fire extinguisher"

A businessman climbs up a beanstalk and sees a beautiful woman who says, "You can have sex with me or you can climb higher to success". He decides to climb higher and sees an even more beautiful woman. The woman says, "You can have sex with me or you can climb higher to success". The businessman passes ever more beautiful women as he continues to climb higher and higher until he reaches the very top. He sees a huge naked man and says, "Who are you?" The huge man replies, "I'm Cess"

Two very old men visit a brothel. The manager thinks that they look so senile that they wouldn't know the difference between a real woman and a blowup doll. After the men have had sex with the blowup dolls, they meet up with each other for a drink to discuss their experience. The first man says, "I'm sure my woman was dead because she didn't move, talk or groan". The second man said, "I'm sure my woman was a witch because when I nibbled her tit, she did a fart and flew out of the window"

A woman placed a dating advert in her local newspaper. She wrote, "I'm looking for a man that won't beat me up, won't run away and is great in bed". The next day, her doorbell rings and a man says, "Hi, I'm James. I don't have any arms so I can't beat you up and I don't have any legs so I can't run away". The woman replies, "How do I know you are great in bed?" James replied, "How do you think I rang the doorbell?"

An airplane is about to crash and a woman stands up, rips her clothes off and shouts, "Before I die, is there a man here that will make me feel like a woman?" A man stood up, took his shirt off and shouted back, "Here, iron this"

A couple had been dating for a few weeks and then the topic of sex came up. The man asked the woman, "How often do you like to have sex?" She replied, "Infrequently". The man scratched his head and said, "Is that one word or two?"

You really have to hand it to the blind prostitute

A mother told her husband, "You'll never guess what I found when I was cleaning our daughters bedroom. I found 2 bottles of beer under her bed. I never even knew that she was drinking alcohol". The father then said, "That's nothing. When I was emptying her bin, I found a condom. I never knew that she had a penis"

A man fancied a woman at work but he had a huge problem. Every time he looked at her, he got an erection so he didn't dare walk over to her. Eventually, he decided to use the computer messaging system to ask her out on a date. That evening, the man strapped his penis to his leg to prevent embarrassing himself. He plucks the courage to knock on her door and she answered the door in just her underwear. He then kicked her in the face

Printed in Great Britain
by Amazon